A Comprehensive Guide to Investment Opportunities

C. P. Kumar
Reiki Healer
Roorkee - 247667, India

Disclaimer

While every effort has been made to ensure the accuracy and completeness of the content in this book, the author cannot guarantee that the information contained herein is error-free, up-to-date, or suitable for every individual circumstance.

The author shall not be held liable or responsible for any errors or omissions in the content of the book, nor for any damages, or losses that may arise from any actions taken based upon the suggestions or contents presented in the book.

Readers are advised to use their own judgment and discretion in applying the information provided in this book, and to consult with qualified professionals before taking any action based on the contents of this book. The author disclaims any and all liability or responsibility for any actions taken or not taken based on the information contained in this book.

DEDICATION

This book is dedicated to all those who have a keen interest in investing and growing their wealth. Whether you are a beginner or an experienced investor, this comprehensive guide has been written to help you understand the different investment opportunities available and make informed decisions to achieve your financial goals.

To all the readers who have taken the time to learn about investing, to all those who have taken risks and had the courage to invest in something new, to all those who have seen the benefits of a diversified portfolio, and to all those who have invested for their future – this book is for you.

May this guide empower you to make smart investment decisions, help you navigate the complex world of investing, and provide you with the knowledge and tools to build a strong and sustainable financial future.

C. P. Kumar

CONTENTS

PREFACE

Investing your money can be a smart and effective way to build wealth and secure your financial future. However, with so many investment opportunities available, it can be overwhelming to know where to start and what options are right for you.

The purpose of this book, "A Comprehensive Guide to Investment Opportunities," is to provide you with a clear and concise overview of the most popular investment opportunities available, and the tools and strategies you need to make informed investment decisions.

In this book, we cover a range of investment opportunities, including stocks, bonds, mutual funds, exchange-traded funds (ETFs), real estate, commodities, gold, forex trading, cryptocurrency, and alternative investments such as hedge funds, private equity, and venture capital.

We also cover essential topics such as risk management, tax planning, portfolio diversification, and retirement planning, which are all critical to successful investing.

It is important to note that the examples and relevant provisions quoted in this book are primarily from the United States. While the principles of investing generally apply across borders, it is crucial for readers to consult the relevant provisions applicable in their own countries. Each country may have its own regulations, laws, and tax considerations that can impact investment opportunities and strategies. We encourage readers to seek advice from local financial professionals and refer to the specific regulations and laws in their respective countries.

Whether you're a beginner looking to start your investment journey or an experienced investor looking to expand your portfolio, this book has something for everyone. We aim to provide you with practical guidance, insights, and tips that you can apply to your investment strategies and make informed decisions.

Investing can be a rewarding experience, but it's important to approach it with caution and knowledge. We hope that this book will serve as a valuable resource and guide to help you navigate the world of investing and make the most of the opportunities available.

C. P. Kumar
Reiki Healer
Former Scientist 'G', National Institute of Hydrology
Roorkee - 247667, India
E-mail: cpkumar@yahoo.com
Web: https://www.angelfire.com/nh/cpkumar/virgo.html

Introduction

Investing is the process of putting money to work in order to grow or increase its value. It is a means of building wealth, achieving financial goals, and securing a comfortable future. Whether you are looking to invest in stocks, bonds, real estate, or other assets, it is important to understand the basics of investing before making any investment decisions. In this article, we will provide an introduction to investing and discuss some of the key concepts and terms you need to know.

Why Invest?

The primary reason people invest is to earn a return on their money. There are many different types of investments, each with its own risk and reward profile. Generally speaking, the higher the risk, the higher the potential reward. Some people invest for the long-term, seeking to build wealth over many years. Others invest for the short-term, looking to make quick profits by buying and selling stocks or other assets.

Another reason people invest is to hedge against inflation. Over time, the cost of goods and services tends to increase, which can erode the purchasing power of your money. By investing in assets that appreciate in value over time, you can help protect your savings against inflation.

Types of Investments

There are many different types of investments, each with its own unique characteristics and risks. Some of the most common types of investments include:

Stocks: Stocks represent ownership in a company and are bought and sold on stock exchanges. Stocks can provide a potential for high returns, but also come with a high level of risk.

Bonds: Bonds are debt securities issued by governments and corporations. They provide a fixed rate of return over a set period of time and are generally considered to be less risky than stocks.

Real Estate: Real estate can be a great long-term investment, providing both rental income and appreciation in value. However, it can also be risky, as it is subject to market fluctuations and may require significant upfront investment.

Mutual Funds: Mutual funds are investment vehicles that pool money from multiple investors to invest in a diversified portfolio of stocks, bonds, or other assets. They offer diversification and professional management, but also come with fees and expenses.

ETFs: Exchange-traded funds (ETFs) are similar to mutual funds in that they provide access to a diversified portfolio of assets. However, ETFs are traded on stock exchanges like individual stocks, and generally have lower fees than mutual funds.

Key Investment Concepts

Before investing, it is important to understand some key investment concepts. These include:

Risk: Risk refers to the potential for loss associated with an investment. All investments carry some level of risk, but some are riskier than others.

Return: Return refers to the profit or loss you make on an investment. The return can be positive or negative and is typically expressed as a percentage.

Diversification: Diversification refers to the practice of spreading your investments across multiple asset classes, sectors, and regions. By diversifying your portfolio, you can reduce your overall risk and increase your potential for long-term returns.

Asset Allocation: Asset allocation refers to the process of dividing your investments among different asset classes, such as stocks, bonds, and real estate. Your asset allocation should be based on your investment goals, risk tolerance, and time horizon.

Rebalancing: Rebalancing refers to the process of adjusting your portfolio to maintain your desired asset allocation. Over time, some assets may perform better than others, which can cause your portfolio to become unbalanced. By periodically rebalancing your portfolio, you can ensure that your investments remain aligned with your goals and risk tolerance.

Conclusion

Investing can be a great way to grow your wealth and achieve your financial goals. However, it is important to understand the basics of investing before getting started. By familiarizing yourself with the different types of investments, key investment concepts, and your personal investment goals and risk tolerance, you can make informed investment decisions that are right for you.

It is also important to remember that investing involves risk and there is no guarantee of returns. Past performance is not indicative of future results, and there are many factors that can impact the value of your investments, such as economic conditions, company performance, and global events.

When investing, it is important to have a long-term perspective and not make investment decisions based on short-term fluctuations in the market. It is also important to have a diversified portfolio that is aligned with your investment goals and risk tolerance.

Lastly, it is always a good idea to consult with a financial advisor before making any investment decisions. A financial advisor can help you assess your investment goals and risk tolerance, and develop a personalized investment strategy that is right for you.

In conclusion, investing can be a powerful tool for building wealth and achieving your financial goals. By understanding the basics of investing, and working with a financial advisor to develop a personalized investment strategy, you can make informed investment decisions that are right for you.

Chapter 2. Risk Management
Essential Tools for Successful Investing

Introduction

Investing can be an excellent way to grow your wealth over time, but it comes with a level of risk. No investment is entirely risk-free, and the market is subject to volatility, which can make it challenging to make sound decisions.

One of the most critical aspects of investing is managing risk effectively. In this article, we will explore some essential tools for risk management that can help you become a successful investor.

What is Risk Management?

Risk management is a process that involves identifying, assessing, and prioritizing potential risks and taking steps to minimize or avoid them. It is a crucial part of investing because it helps investors make informed decisions about their investments and reduce the chances of significant financial losses.

Effective risk management involves understanding the potential risks associated with different investments, developing a strategy to mitigate those risks, and monitoring the performance of your investments over time to ensure that they are meeting your expectations.

Essential Tools for Successful Investing

1. Diversification

Diversification is a strategy that involves spreading your investments across different asset classes, industries, and geographical regions to reduce the risk of losses in any one investment. It is an effective tool for managing risk because it helps to minimize the impact of market volatility on your portfolio.

For example, if you only invest in one type of asset, such as stocks, you are more vulnerable to market fluctuations that can affect the value of your entire portfolio. However, if you invest in a mix of assets, such as stocks, bonds, and real estate, you can reduce your overall risk because the performance of each asset class is unlikely to be correlated.

2. Asset Allocation

Asset allocation is the process of dividing your investment portfolio among different asset classes, such as stocks, bonds, and cash, based on your investment goals, risk tolerance, and time horizon. It is an essential tool for managing risk because it helps to ensure that your portfolio is appropriately balanced and aligned with your investment objectives.

Asset allocation can help to reduce the risk of losses in your portfolio because it ensures that you are not overly exposed to any one asset class. For example, if you have a long time horizon and are willing to accept higher risk, you may allocate a higher percentage of your portfolio to stocks. However, if you have a shorter time horizon or are more risk-averse, you may allocate more to bonds or cash.

3. Stop-Loss Orders

Stop-loss orders are a type of order that investors can use to limit their losses in a particular investment. It is an effective tool for managing risk because it allows investors to set a predetermined price at which they will sell a security automatically.

For example, if you buy a stock at $50 and set a stop-loss order at $45, if the stock price falls to $45, your shares will be automatically sold, limiting your potential losses. Stop-loss orders can help investors avoid emotional decision-making and protect their investments from significant losses.

4. Risk Assessment

Risk assessment is the process of evaluating the potential risks associated with different investments. It is an essential tool for managing risk because it helps investors make informed decisions about their investments and avoid unnecessary risks.

When assessing the risk of an investment, investors should consider factors such as the industry, the company's financial health, and the overall market conditions. By evaluating these factors, investors can gain a better understanding of the potential risks associated with an investment and make more informed decisions.

5. Hedging Strategies

Hedging strategies are a set of techniques used by investors to reduce the risk of losses in their portfolio. They involve taking an opposite position to a particular investment, such as buying a put option or shorting a stock.

For example, if you own a stock that you believe is likely to decrease in value, you could buy a put option, which would give you the right to sell the stock at a predetermined price. If the stock price falls below the predetermined price, you can exercise the put option, limiting your losses. Hedging strategies can be complex and involve additional costs, but they can be effective in managing risk.

6. Regular Portfolio Rebalancing

Regular portfolio rebalancing is the process of adjusting your portfolio's asset allocation to ensure that it remains aligned with your investment objectives and risk tolerance. It is an essential tool for managing risk because it helps to ensure that your portfolio is appropriately balanced and diversified.

For example, if your portfolio's target allocation is 60% stocks and 40% bonds, and the stock market has performed well, your stock allocation may have increased to 70%. By rebalancing your portfolio, you would sell some of your stocks and buy bonds to return to your target allocation, reducing your overall risk.

7. Investment Horizon

The investment horizon is the length of time that an investor plans to hold an investment. It is an essential tool for managing risk because it can help investors determine the appropriate level of risk for their portfolio.

Investors with a longer investment horizon, such as those investing for retirement, may be willing to accept higher levels of risk because they have more time to recover from potential losses. Conversely, investors with a shorter investment horizon, such as those saving for a down payment on a home, may be more risk-averse and choose investments with lower risk.

Conclusion

Managing risk is an essential part of successful investing. By using the tools discussed in this article, investors can reduce the risk of losses and make more informed decisions about their investments. However, it is important to remember that investing always involves a level of risk, and no strategy can guarantee a profit or protect against losses.

As an investor, it is essential to do your research, consult with a financial advisor, and develop a risk management strategy that aligns with your investment objectives and risk tolerance. By doing so, you can minimize your risk and increase your chances of achieving your long-term financial goals.

Chapter 3. Tax Planning for Investors
Maximizing Returns and Minimizing Liabilities

Introduction

Tax planning is an essential part of any investment strategy. It can help investors maximize returns by minimizing tax liabilities and ensuring compliance with tax laws. In this article, we will discuss the importance of tax planning for investors and provide some tips on how to maximize returns and minimize liabilities.

Why Tax Planning is Important for Investors

Investors are always looking for ways to maximize their returns. However, taxes can eat into their profits, reducing the returns on their investments. This is where tax planning comes in. Tax planning involves taking steps to minimize tax liabilities and ensure compliance with tax laws.

Tax planning is essential for investors for several reasons. Firstly, it can help investors maximize their after-tax returns. By reducing tax liabilities, investors can keep more of their profits, increasing their returns. Secondly, tax planning can help investors manage their cash flow. By planning for taxes, investors can ensure that they have sufficient cash to pay taxes when due, avoiding penalties and interest charges. Finally, tax planning can help investors avoid tax-related risks, such as audits and penalties.

Tips for Maximizing Returns and Minimizing Liabilities

1. Understand the Tax Laws

The first step in tax planning is to understand the tax laws. Investors need to be familiar with the tax rules and regulations that apply to their investments. They also need to be aware of any changes in the tax laws that may affect their investments. For example, the tax laws that apply to real estate investments may differ from those that apply to stocks and bonds.

It is also important to understand the tax implications of different investment strategies. For example, investing in dividend-paying stocks may result in higher tax liabilities than investing in stocks that do not pay dividends.

2. Use Tax-Advantaged Accounts

Tax-advantaged accounts, such as Individual Retirement Accounts (IRAs) and 401(k) plans (applicable in the United States), can help investors minimize their tax liabilities. Contributions to these accounts are tax-deductible, and the earnings grow tax-free until withdrawn. This can result in significant tax savings over the long term.

Investors should also consider using tax-advantaged accounts for specific types of investments. For example, real estate investors can use a Self-Directed IRA (applicable in the United States) to invest in real estate, which can provide tax advantages.

3. Consider Tax-Loss Harvesting

Tax-loss harvesting involves selling investments that have declined in value to offset capital gains. This can help investors minimize their tax liabilities while still maintaining their investment positions. Investors can use tax-loss harvesting to offset gains in one year or carry forward losses to offset gains in future years.

4. Minimize Capital Gains Taxes

Investors can minimize their capital gains taxes by holding investments for more than one year. This will qualify them for long-term capital gains tax rates, which are lower than short-term capital gains tax rates. Investors can also consider selling investments that have appreciated in value in years when they expect to have lower taxable income.

5. Be Aware of Alternative Minimum Tax

The Alternative Minimum Tax (AMT) is a separate tax system (applicable in the United States) that is designed to ensure that high-income taxpayers pay their fair share of taxes. It applies to taxpayers whose income exceeds certain thresholds. Investors need to be aware of the AMT and plan accordingly. They may need to adjust their investment strategies to minimize their AMT liability.

6. Consider Tax-Efficient Investments

Investors can consider investing in tax-efficient investments, such as exchange-traded funds (ETFs) and index funds. These investments are designed to minimize tax liabilities by minimizing turnover and maximizing tax efficiency. They can also provide diversification benefits and lower fees than actively managed funds.

7. Consult with a Tax Professional

Investors should consult with a tax professional to develop a tax planning strategy that is tailored to their individual needs. A tax professional can provide valuable insights into the tax laws and regulations that apply to specific investments and help investors identify tax planning opportunities. They can also help investors stay up-to-date on changes in the tax laws and regulations.

Conclusion

Tax planning is an essential part of any investment strategy. It can help investors maximize their returns by minimizing tax liabilities and ensuring compliance with tax laws. By understanding the tax laws, using tax-advantaged accounts, considering tax-loss harvesting, minimizing capital gains taxes, being aware of the AMT, considering tax-efficient investments, and consulting with a tax professional, investors can develop a tax planning strategy that maximizes returns and minimizes liabilities.

Chapter 4. Building a Diversified Investment Portfolio

Balancing Risk and Reward

Introduction

Investing is one of the most important activities in personal finance, but it can also be one of the most challenging. With so many investment options available, it can be overwhelming to know where to start. One strategy that can help investors reduce risk and maximize returns is diversification. In this article, we will explore the concept of diversification and provide some tips for building a diversified investment portfolio that balances risk and reward.

What is Diversification?

Diversification is the process of investing in a variety of assets to reduce risk. The idea behind diversification is that if one asset class performs poorly, another asset class may perform well, thereby balancing out the losses. The goal of diversification is not only to reduce risk but also to maximize returns. By investing in a variety of assets, investors can take advantage of the potential for high returns in some asset classes while mitigating the risk of losses in others.

Asset Classes

To build a diversified investment portfolio, investors need to invest in different asset classes. The four main asset classes are stocks, bonds, cash, and real estate.

1. Stocks: Stocks are shares of ownership in a company. Stocks are one of the most common investment options, and they can be bought and sold easily. Stocks are known for their potential for high returns, but they are also associated with high risk.

2. Bonds: Bonds are debt securities issued by companies or governments. When an investor buys a bond, they are essentially loaning money to the issuer. Bonds are known for their stability and low risk, but they also offer lower returns than stocks.

3. Cash: Cash includes savings accounts, money market funds, and other cash equivalents. Cash is the least risky asset class, but it also offers the lowest returns.

4. Real Estate: Real estate includes physical property such as houses, apartments, and commercial buildings. Real estate can offer both income and capital appreciation, but it is also associated with higher risk and requires a significant investment.

Risk vs. Reward

When building a diversified investment portfolio, investors need to balance risk and reward. The amount of risk an investor is willing to take will depend on their personal goals and risk tolerance. Investors who are willing to take on more risk may choose to invest more heavily in stocks or real estate, while investors who are more risk-averse may choose to invest more heavily in bonds or cash.

It is important to note that higher returns are typically associated with higher risk. Investors who are looking for high returns should be prepared to accept a higher level of risk, while investors who are more focused on preserving capital should be prepared to accept lower returns.

Asset Allocation

Asset allocation is the process of dividing an investment portfolio among different asset classes. The goal of asset allocation is to create a diversified portfolio that balances risk and reward. There is no one-size-fits-all approach to asset allocation, as the optimal allocation will depend on an investor's goals, risk tolerance, and time horizon.

One popular approach to asset allocation is the "60/40" rule, which suggests that investors allocate 60% of their portfolio to stocks and 40% to bonds. This rule can be adjusted based on an investor's personal circumstances and risk tolerance.

Another approach to asset allocation is to use a target-date fund. Target-date funds are designed to adjust the allocation of assets based on an investor's target retirement date. The allocation of assets becomes more conservative as the target retirement date approaches.

Diversification within Asset Classes

Diversification is not only important across asset classes but also within asset classes. For example, within the stock asset class, investors can diversify their holdings by investing in different sectors, such as technology, healthcare, and energy. Within the bond asset class, investors can diversify their holdings by investing in bonds with different maturities and credit ratings.

Diversification within asset classes can help to reduce the risk of loss due to a single stock or bond. For example, if an investor has a portfolio consisting of only technology stocks and the technology sector experiences a downturn, the entire portfolio could suffer significant losses. However, if the investor had diversified their holdings by investing in stocks across different sectors, the losses would have been mitigated.

Rebalancing

Rebalancing is the process of adjusting the allocation of assets in a portfolio. Over time, the performance of different asset classes can change, leading to a portfolio that is no longer balanced. Rebalancing allows investors to adjust their portfolios back to their target allocation.

Rebalancing can be done on a set schedule, such as quarterly or annually, or when the allocation of assets deviates significantly from the target allocation. Rebalancing can help investors maintain a balanced portfolio and reduce the risk of losses due to overexposure to a single asset class.

Conclusion

Diversification is a key strategy for building a successful investment portfolio that balances risk and reward. By investing in different asset classes and diversifying within those asset classes, investors can reduce their overall risk while maximizing returns. Asset allocation, diversification within asset classes, and rebalancing are all important components of building a diversified investment portfolio.

It is important for investors to remember that there is no one-size-fits-all approach to investing. Each investor's circumstances and goals are unique, and their investment strategy should reflect that. It is always a good idea for investors to consult with a financial advisor before making any investment decisions to ensure that their investment strategy aligns with their personal goals and risk tolerance.

Chapter 5. Shares
A Comprehensive Guide for Beginners

Introduction

Investing in shares, also known as stocks or equities, can be a profitable way to grow your wealth. But if you're new to the world of investing, it can also be intimidating and confusing. In this comprehensive guide, we'll walk you through the basics of shares, including what they are, how to invest in them, and some tips for getting started.

What are Shares?

Shares are a type of financial instrument that represent ownership in a company. When you buy a share, you are buying a small piece of the company and become a shareholder. As a shareholder, you are entitled to a portion of the company's profits, known as dividends, and the right to vote on certain matters at the company's annual general meeting (AGM).

Shares are traded on stock exchanges, such as the New York Stock Exchange (NYSE) or the London Stock Exchange (LSE). The price of a share is determined by supply and demand in the market, and can fluctuate based on various factors such as the company's financial performance, news events, and overall market conditions.

How to Invest in Shares

There are several ways to invest in shares, including through a broker, a robo-advisor, or directly through the company itself.

1. Broker

A broker is a financial professional who helps you buy and sell shares. They typically charge a commission or a fee for their services, which can vary depending on the broker and the type of account you have. Some popular online brokers include Robinhood, E*TRADE, and TD Ameritrade (online brokerage firms based in the United States).

When choosing a broker, it's important to consider factors such as fees, account minimums, and the types of investment options available. Some brokers also offer additional features such as research tools, educational resources, and investment advice.

2. Robo-Advisor

A robo-advisor is a digital investment platform that uses algorithms and computer models to manage your investments. Robo-advisors typically charge lower fees than traditional brokers and offer a more hands-off approach to investing. Some popular robo-advisors include Betterment, Wealthfront, and Personal Capital (based in the United States).

When using a robo-advisor, you'll typically answer a series of questions about your investment goals, risk tolerance, and time horizon. The robo-advisor will then create a diversified portfolio of shares based on your answers and automatically rebalance your portfolio as needed.

3. Direct Purchase Plans

Some companies offer direct purchase plans (DPPs), which allow you to buy shares directly from the company. DPPs typically have lower fees than brokers and can be a good option if you're interested in investing in a specific company.

To participate in a DPP, you'll need to open an account with the company's transfer agent and meet any eligibility requirements. You may also be required to make a minimum initial investment.

Tips for Investing in Shares

1. Diversify Your Portfolio

Diversification is key to successful investing. By spreading your money across a variety of shares and other assets, you can help reduce your risk and increase your chances of long-term growth.

One way to diversify your portfolio is to invest in shares across different industries and sectors. This can help you avoid putting all your eggs in one basket and protect your portfolio from downturns in any one sector.

2. Invest for the Long-Term

Investing in shares is a long-term game. While there may be short-term fluctuations in the market, history has shown that the stock market tends to rise over time. By staying invested for the long-term, you can give your portfolio time to weather these ups and downs and potentially earn higher returns.

3. Do Your Research

Before investing in any share, it's important to do your research. This can involve reading the company's financial statements, researching its industry and competitors, and analyzing the broader market trends.

It's also a good idea to stay up-to-date on any news or events that may impact the company's stock price. For example, if a company announces a major new product or experiences a scandal, this could cause the stock price to rise or fall.

4. Be Prepared for Volatility

Investing in shares involves some level of risk, and it's important to be prepared for volatility in the market. Share prices can fluctuate dramatically based on a variety of factors, including economic conditions, political events, and company-specific news.

While it can be tempting to panic and sell your shares during a downturn, it's important to stay the course and stick to your long-term investment strategy. By keeping a diversified portfolio and investing for the long-term, you can help reduce the impact of market volatility on your portfolio.

5. Consider Investing in Index Funds

If you're new to investing or don't have the time or resources to research individual shares, index funds can be a good option. An index fund is a type of mutual fund or exchange-traded fund (ETF) that tracks a specific stock market index, such as the S&P 500 or the Dow Jones Industrial Average.

By investing in an index fund, you can gain exposure to a broad range of shares across different industries and sectors. This can help you diversify your portfolio and potentially earn higher returns over the long-term.

Conclusion

Investing in shares can be a rewarding way to grow your wealth over the long-term. By understanding the basics of shares, how to invest in them, and some tips for getting started, you can make informed decisions and build a diversified portfolio that meets your investment goals.

Remember to do your research, diversify your portfolio, and invest for the long-term. And don't forget to be prepared for volatility in the market – by staying the course and sticking to your investment strategy, you can help ensure long-term success in your investment journey.

Chapter 6. Bonds

A Steady Income Stream for Long-Term Investors

Introduction

Investing can be intimidating for those who are new to the game. With so many options available, it can be difficult to decide where to put your money to work. One popular investment option is bonds, which are a type of fixed-income security that can provide investors with a steady income stream over the long term. In this article, we'll discuss what bonds are, how they work, and why they can be a great choice for long-term investors.

What are Bonds?

In simple terms, a bond is a loan made by an investor to an entity such as a government or corporation. When an entity wants to raise money, they can issue bonds to investors who purchase them. The entity promises to pay back the amount borrowed, plus interest, over a set period of time.

Bonds are generally considered to be less risky than stocks because they are backed by the issuer's ability to pay back the loan. In other words, if a company issues bonds and then goes bankrupt, the bondholders are typically paid back before the company's shareholders. This means that bonds are generally considered to be a safer investment than stocks, although they typically offer lower returns.

How do Bonds Work?

Bonds are typically issued with a face value, or par value, which is the amount that the investor pays to purchase the bond. For example, a bond with a face value of $1,000 may be sold for $950, which means the investor is effectively loaning $950 to the issuer. The issuer promises to pay back the full $1,000 when the bond matures, plus interest over the life of the bond.

The interest rate paid on a bond is known as the coupon rate, and it is usually fixed when the bond is issued. For example, a bond with a face value of $1,000 and a coupon rate of 5% would pay the investor $50 per year in interest. The length of time until the bond matures is known as the term, and it can vary from a few months to several decades.

The face value of a bond is the amount the issuer is obligated to repay at maturity. Whether the bond was purchased at a discount or premium does not directly affect the capital gain or loss realized at maturity. Capital gains or losses in the context of bonds typically arise from selling the bond before maturity and realizing a difference between the selling price and the purchase price.

Why are Bonds a Good Choice for Long-Term Investors?

While bonds may offer lower returns than stocks, they can be a great choice for long-term investors who prioritize stability and a steady income stream. Here are a few reasons why:

1. Fixed Income: Bonds provide a fixed income stream to investors, which means that investors can count on a predictable amount of interest payments over the life of the bond. This can be particularly attractive to retirees or those who are looking for a reliable source of income.

2. Diversification: Adding bonds to an investment portfolio can help diversify risk. This is because the bond market

tends to behave differently than the stock market. When the stock market is volatile, bonds can provide a stable counterbalance. This can help reduce the overall risk of a portfolio and potentially improve returns over the long term.

3. Lower Risk: Bonds are generally considered to be less risky than stocks. This is because bondholders have priority over shareholders when it comes to getting paid back in the event of bankruptcy or liquidation. While there is still some risk involved with investing in bonds, it is generally lower than with stocks.

4. Capital Preservation: Bonds can help preserve capital by providing a stable source of income and a return of principal at maturity. This can be particularly important for investors who are looking to protect their wealth and preserve their purchasing power over the long term.

5. Inflation Protection: Some types of bonds, such as Treasury Inflation-Protected Securities (TIPS), are designed to protect investors from inflation. TIPS pay a fixed interest rate, but the principal value of the bond is adjusted for inflation over time. This means that investors can count on a predictable return that will keep pace with inflation.

Conclusion

Investing in bonds can be a great choice for long-term investors who prioritize stability and a steady income stream. While bonds may offer lower returns than stocks, they also offer lower risk and can help diversify an investment portfolio. Whether you are a retiree looking for a reliable source of income, or a young investor looking to build wealth over the long term, bonds can be a valuable addition to your investment strategy. As with any investment, it is important to do your research and consult with a financial advisor before making any decisions.

Chapter 7. Mutual Funds
A Diversified Approach to Investing

Introduction

Investing is an important aspect of personal finance, and it is essential for building long-term wealth. However, with so many investment options available, it can be overwhelming to decide which investment option to choose. Mutual funds are a popular investment option, and they offer a diversified approach to investing. This article will discuss mutual funds and why they are a great way to invest.

What are Mutual Funds?

Mutual funds are investment vehicles that pool money from different investors to invest in a variety of assets such as stocks, bonds, and money market instruments. Mutual funds are managed by professional fund managers who use the pooled money to buy a diverse range of securities to achieve the fund's investment objective. The fund manager is responsible for making investment decisions and managing the fund's assets.

Types of Mutual Funds

There are different types of mutual funds, and each type has a unique investment objective. Here are some of the common types of mutual funds:

Equity Funds: These funds invest in stocks of companies. Equity funds can be further classified into large-cap funds, mid-cap funds, and small-cap funds based on the market capitalization of the companies in which they invest.

Debt Funds: These funds invest in fixed-income securities such as bonds, debentures, and government securities. Debt funds can be further classified into short-term funds, long-term funds, and dynamic bond funds based on the maturity of the securities in which they invest.

Hybrid Funds: These funds invest in both equity and debt instruments. Hybrid funds can be further classified into balanced funds, conservative funds, and aggressive funds based on the proportion of equity and debt instruments in their portfolio.

Index Funds: These funds invest in a basket of securities that mimic a particular market index such as the Nifty 50 or the BSE Sensex. Index funds aim to replicate the returns of the underlying index.

Benefits of Investing in Mutual Funds

Diversification: Mutual funds offer diversification by investing in a variety of securities. Diversification helps to reduce the risk of loss as the fund's assets are spread across multiple securities and sectors.

Professional Management: Mutual funds are managed by professional fund managers who have the expertise and experience to make investment decisions. The fund manager's responsibility is to analyze the market and make investment decisions based on the fund's investment objective.

Liquidity: Mutual funds are liquid investments, which means that investors can buy or sell their units at any time. Mutual funds are listed on the stock exchange, and investors can sell their units back to the fund house or on the stock exchange.

Affordability: Mutual funds offer an affordable way to invest in a diversified portfolio of securities. Investors can start with a small amount of money and gradually increase their investment over time.

Tax Benefits: Mutual funds offer tax benefits to investors. Equity funds held for more than one year are considered long-term capital gains and are taxed at a lower rate than short-term capital gains. Debt funds held for more than three years are also taxed at a lower rate than short-term capital gains.

How to Invest in Mutual Funds

Investing in mutual funds is a simple and straightforward process. Here are the steps to invest in mutual funds:

Step 1: Choose a fund house: Choose a reputable fund house that offers a range of mutual funds with a good track record.

Step 2: Choose a fund: Choose a mutual fund that aligns with your investment objective and risk profile.

Step 3: Complete KYC: Complete your Know Your Customer (KYC) process with the fund house or a KYC registration agency.

Step 4: Choose an investment mode: Choose an investment mode based on your preference. You can invest in mutual funds through a lump sum investment or a Systematic Investment Plan (SIP).

Step 5: Make the Investment: Once you have completed the KYC process and chosen your investment mode, you can make the investment through the fund house's website or through a distributor.

Tips for Investing in Mutual Funds

1. Define your investment objective: It is important to define your investment objective before investing in mutual funds. Your investment objective can be short-term or long-term, and it should align with your financial goals.

2. Assess your risk profile: Assess your risk profile before investing in mutual funds. Your risk profile will determine the type of mutual funds you should invest in. If you are a conservative investor, you should consider debt funds, while if you are an aggressive investor, you should consider equity funds.

3. Choose a reputable fund house: Choose a reputable fund house that has a good track record of performance and has been in the market for a long time.

4. Diversify your portfolio: Diversify your portfolio by investing in different types of mutual funds. This will help to reduce the risk of loss and ensure that your portfolio is balanced.

5. Monitor your investments: It is important to monitor your investments and review your portfolio regularly. This will help you to make informed decisions and ensure that your portfolio is aligned with your investment objective.

Conclusion

Mutual funds offer a diversified approach to investing, and they are a great way to build long-term wealth. Mutual funds offer professional management, diversification, liquidity, affordability, and tax benefits. Investors can choose from different types of mutual funds based on their investment objective and risk profile. Investing in mutual funds is a simple and straightforward process, and investors can start with a small amount of money and gradually increase their investment over time. It is important to define your investment objective, assess your risk profile, choose a reputable fund house, diversify your portfolio, and monitor your investments to ensure that your portfolio is aligned with your investment objective.

Chapter 8. Exchange-Traded Funds (ETFs)

An Overview of Investing in Low-Cost, Diversified Portfolios

Introduction

Exchange-traded funds (ETFs) have gained significant popularity among investors in recent years due to their low cost, diversification, and flexibility. ETFs are investment funds that trade on stock exchanges, similar to stocks. They offer investors exposure to a diversified portfolio of assets, such as stocks, bonds, or commodities, at a low cost compared to actively managed mutual funds. In this article, we will provide an overview of ETFs, their benefits, and how to invest in them.

What are ETFs?

ETFs are investment funds that hold a basket of assets, such as stocks, bonds, or commodities, and trade on stock exchanges. They are similar to mutual funds, but ETFs are traded on an exchange like stocks. ETFs are designed to track the performance of an underlying index, such as the S&P 500, the Dow Jones Industrial Average, or the NASDAQ.

ETFs are typically passively managed, which means they do not rely on a fund manager to actively buy and sell stocks in the portfolio. Instead, they track a predetermined index, so the portfolio of assets in an ETF will be similar to the assets in the underlying index.

Benefits of Investing in ETFs

There are several benefits to investing in ETFs, including:

1. Low Cost: ETFs are typically low-cost investments, with lower management fees than actively managed mutual funds. This is because ETFs are passively managed and do not require as much effort to buy and sell stocks as actively managed funds.

2. Diversification: ETFs offer investors exposure to a diversified portfolio of assets, which can help reduce the risk of losses from individual stocks or sectors. By investing in an ETF, investors gain exposure to a basket of stocks or other assets rather than buying individual stocks.

3. Flexibility: ETFs trade on stock exchanges like stocks, so investors can buy and sell them throughout the trading day. This allows investors to adjust their portfolio quickly and easily.

4. Transparency: ETFs are transparent investments, and investors can see the underlying assets in the fund. ETFs also provide daily updates on their holdings, so investors can see how their investments are performing.

How to Invest in ETFs

Investing in ETFs is similar to investing in stocks. Investors can buy and sell ETFs through a brokerage account, either online or with a traditional broker. There are several steps investors can take to invest in ETFs:

1. Determine Your Investment Goals: Before investing in ETFs, investors should determine their investment goals,

risk tolerance, and time horizon. This will help them choose the right ETFs to meet their investment objectives.

2. Choose an ETF: Investors can choose from a wide range of ETFs that track different indexes, sectors, or asset classes. They should choose an ETF that aligns with their investment goals and risk tolerance.

3. Open a Brokerage Account: Investors will need to open a brokerage account to buy and sell ETFs. They can choose from a variety of online brokers or traditional brokers.

4. Place Your Trade: Once investors have chosen an ETF and opened a brokerage account, they can place a trade to buy the ETF. Investors can choose to buy a specific number of shares or a dollar amount of the ETF.

5. Monitor Your Investment: Investors should monitor their ETF investments regularly to ensure they are meeting their investment goals. They should also keep an eye on the performance of the underlying index and make adjustments to their portfolio as needed.

Types of ETFs

There are several types of ETFs that investors can choose from, including:

1. Equity ETFs: Equity ETFs track a specific index, such as the S&P 500, or a specific sector, such as technology or healthcare. They invest in stocks of companies within the index or sector.

2. Fixed-Income ETFs: Fixed-income ETFs invest in bonds and other fixed-income securities, such as Treasury bonds, corporate bonds, or municipal bonds.

3. Commodity ETFs: Commodity ETFs invest in commodities such as gold, silver, or oil. They can either invest directly in the underlying commodity or invest in futures contracts or other derivatives.

4. Currency ETFs: Currency ETFs invest in currencies, such as the US dollar or the Euro. They can either hold the underlying currency or invest in derivatives such as currency futures or options.

5. Alternative ETFs: Alternative ETFs invest in alternative assets such as real estate, commodities, or currencies. They are designed to provide exposure to non-traditional asset classes.

Risks of Investing in ETFs

While ETFs offer several benefits, there are also some risks to consider. Some of the risks of investing in ETFs include:

1. Market Risk: Like all investments, ETFs are subject to market risk. This means that if the underlying index or asset class performs poorly, the ETF will also perform poorly.

2. Liquidity Risk: While ETFs trade like stocks, some ETFs may have low trading volumes, which can make it difficult to buy and sell them at the desired price.

3. Tracking Error: While most ETFs are designed to track the performance of an underlying index, there may be slight tracking errors due to factors such as fees, expenses, or market conditions.

4. Concentration Risk: Some ETFs may be heavily concentrated in a particular sector, industry, or asset class. This can increase the risk of losses if that sector or asset class performs poorly.

Conclusion

ETFs are an increasingly popular investment option for investors due to their low cost, diversification, and flexibility. They offer exposure to a wide range of assets, such as stocks, bonds, commodities, and currencies, and are designed to track the performance of an underlying index. Investors can choose from a variety of ETFs to meet their investment goals and risk tolerance. While ETFs offer several benefits, investors should also be aware of the risks and ensure they understand the underlying index or asset class before investing.

Chapter 9. Debt Funds

A Safe Investment Option for Risk-Averse Investors

Introduction

Investing in debt funds has become an increasingly popular choice among investors who are risk-averse. This is because debt funds offer a relatively safer investment option as compared to equity funds, and also provide regular income in the form of interest payouts. In this article, we will explore what debt funds are, how they work, and why they are a safe investment option for risk-averse investors.

What are Debt Funds?

Debt funds are a type of mutual fund that invests in fixed income securities such as bonds, debentures, and other debt instruments issued by governments, corporates, or financial institutions. Debt funds generate returns through interest income and capital appreciation. The interest income is generated from the interest paid by the issuers of the underlying debt securities, and the capital appreciation is generated from the increase in the price of the underlying securities.

How do Debt Funds Work?

Debt funds are managed by professional fund managers who invest the corpus of the fund in a diversified portfolio of debt instruments. The fund manager decides the allocation of the portfolio based on the investment objective of the fund, the prevailing market conditions, and the credit quality of the underlying securities. Debt funds are classified based on the maturity profile of the underlying securities, i.e., short-term, medium-term, and long-term debt funds.

Short-term debt funds invest in debt securities with a maturity of up to one year, while medium-term debt funds invest in securities with a maturity of one to three years. Long-term debt funds invest in securities with a maturity of more than three years. The investment objective of debt funds can be either to generate regular income or to provide capital appreciation over the long term.

Why are Debt Funds a Safe Investment Option for Risk-Averse Investors?

1. Lower Risk Profile: Debt funds are considered to be a relatively safer investment option as compared to equity funds. This is because debt funds invest in fixed income securities that offer a fixed rate of return. The interest income earned by debt funds is relatively stable, and the chances of capital loss are lower as compared to equity funds.

2. Diversification: Debt funds provide diversification across a wide range of debt instruments, such as government securities, corporate bonds, and other debt instruments. This diversification helps to reduce the risk of default as the fund manager can spread the investments across various issuers and maturities. This ensures that even if one issuer defaults on its payment, the impact on the overall portfolio is limited.

3. Professional Management: Debt funds are managed by professional fund managers who have the expertise and knowledge to select the right debt instruments. The fund

manager analyses the credit quality of the underlying securities, the economic environment, and the interest rate scenario before making investment decisions. This professional management ensures that the fund is managed efficiently and effectively, thereby reducing the risk for investors.

4. Regular Income: Debt funds provide regular income in the form of interest payouts. This is particularly attractive for investors who are looking for a steady stream of income. The interest payouts are generally higher than the interest rates offered by banks on fixed deposits, making them an attractive investment option for risk-averse investors.

5. Liquidity: Debt funds offer high liquidity as investors can buy and sell units of the fund on any business day. This provides flexibility to investors who may need to liquidate their investments quickly in case of any emergency.

6. Tax Efficiency: Debt funds are considered to be tax-efficient as compared to other fixed income investments such as fixed deposits. Long-term capital gains from debt funds are taxed at a lower rate of 20%, while interest income is taxed as per the individual's tax bracket. This tax efficiency helps to improve the overall returns from the investment.

Risks Associated with Debt Funds

While debt funds are considered to be a relatively safer investment option, they are not completely risk-free. Some of the risks associated with debt funds include:

1. Interest Rate Risk: Debt funds are exposed to interest rate risk as the value of the underlying securities can be

impacted by changes in interest rates. If interest rates rise, the value of the securities held by the fund may fall, resulting in a decline in the net asset value (NAV) of the fund.

2. Credit Risk: Debt funds are also exposed to credit risk, which is the risk of default by the issuer of the underlying securities. If the issuer defaults on its payment obligations, the value of the securities held by the fund may decline, resulting in a decline in the NAV of the fund.

3. Liquidity Risk: Debt funds may also face liquidity risk, which is the risk of not being able to sell the securities held by the fund in the market. This can happen if there is a sudden demand for redemption by investors, and the fund manager is not able to sell the securities at a reasonable price to meet the redemption requirements.

Conclusion

Debt funds are a safe investment option for risk-averse investors as they offer a relatively stable and predictable return. They also provide diversification, professional management, regular income, high liquidity, and tax efficiency. However, investors should be aware of the risks associated with debt funds, such as interest rate risk, credit risk, and liquidity risk. It is important for investors to consult with a financial advisor before investing in debt funds to understand their investment objectives, risk tolerance, and investment horizon.

Chapter 10. Real Estate

An Overview of Investing in Immovable Property

Introduction

Real estate investing involves the purchase, ownership, management, rental, and/or sale of property for profit. It is a popular investment option due to its potential for long-term appreciation and passive income. However, investing in real estate can be a complex process that requires careful consideration and planning.

In this article, we will provide an overview of investing in real estate, including the benefits and risks of investing in immovable property, the different types of real estate investments, and tips for success.

Benefits of Investing in Real Estate

There are several benefits to investing in real estate, including:

1. Cash Flow: Real estate can provide a steady stream of passive income through rental income. When you purchase a property, you can rent it out to tenants, which can generate monthly cash flow.

2. Appreciation: Real estate generally appreciates in value over time. This means that if you purchase a property today, it could be worth significantly more in the future, allowing you to sell it for a profit.

3. Tax Benefits: Real estate investors can take advantage of several tax benefits, such as deductions for mortgage interest, property taxes, and depreciation.

4. Diversification: Investing in real estate can help diversify your investment portfolio, reducing overall risk.

5. Control: Unlike other investment options, real estate allows investors to have more control over their investment. Investors can make decisions regarding property management, renovations, and pricing.

Risks of Investing in Real Estate

While there are several benefits to investing in real estate, there are also risks to consider, including:

1. Market Fluctuations: Real estate prices can be volatile, and market fluctuations can have a significant impact on the value of your investment.

2. Expenses: Investing in real estate can be expensive. In addition to the cost of purchasing a property, there are also ongoing expenses, such as property taxes, maintenance, and insurance.

3. Risk of Vacancy: If you are unable to find tenants for your property, you may experience a loss of income.

4. Legal and Regulatory Risks: Real estate investors need to be aware of the various laws and regulations that govern real estate investments. Failure to comply with these laws can result in legal and financial consequences.

Types of Real Estate Investments

There are several types of real estate investments, each with its own benefits and risks.

1. Residential Real Estate: This includes single-family homes, condos, townhouses, and multi-family properties. Residential real estate is often purchased for rental income or as a primary residence.

2. Commercial Real Estate: This includes office buildings, retail spaces, warehouses, and other commercial properties. Commercial real estate is often purchased for rental income or for business use.

3. Industrial Real Estate: This includes properties such as factories, distribution centers, and storage facilities. Industrial real estate is often purchased for rental income or for business use.

4. Real Estate Investment Trusts (REITs): A REIT is a type of investment that allows investors to own shares in a portfolio of real estate properties. REITs provide a way for investors to invest in real estate without the hassle of property management.

Tips for Success

Investing in real estate can be a complex process, but there are several tips that can help ensure success.

1. Do Your Research: Before investing in a property, it is important to research the market, the property itself, and any potential risks or challenges.

2. Have a Plan: Develop a plan for how you will manage the property, including how you will finance the investment, how you will find tenants, and how you will handle maintenance and repairs.

3. Invest for the Long-Term: Real estate investing is a long-term game. It is important to have a long-term strategy in place and to be patient as you wait for your investment to appreciate in value.

4. Diversify Your Portfolio: While real estate can be a great investment option, it is important to diversify your portfolio to reduce risk. Consider investing in other asset classes, such as stocks or bonds.

5. Build a Team: Real estate investing often requires the help of professionals, such as real estate agents, attorneys, and property managers. Build a team of trusted professionals who can help you navigate the process.

6. Manage Risk: Real estate investing comes with risks, but there are ways to manage these risks. Consider purchasing insurance, diversifying your investments, and being aware of potential market fluctuations.

7. Be Financially Prepared: Investing in real estate can be expensive, and it is important to be financially prepared. Have a solid financial plan in place, including a budget and emergency fund.

Conclusion

Investing in real estate can be a great way to build wealth and generate passive income. However, it is important to understand the benefits and risks of investing in immovable property, as well as the different types of real estate investments available.

By doing your research, developing a plan, diversifying your portfolio, and managing risk, you can increase your chances of success as a real estate investor. With careful consideration and planning, real estate can be a lucrative investment option for those willing to put in the time and effort.

Chapter 11. Commodities

Investing in Physical Assets for Diversification and Inflation Protection

Introduction

Investing in physical commodities has become an increasingly popular strategy for diversifying investment portfolios and protecting against inflation. Commodities are raw materials that are either consumed directly or used in the production of goods and services. Examples of commodities include precious metals like gold and silver, energy sources like oil and natural gas, and agricultural products like corn and soybeans. In this article, we will explore the benefits of investing in commodities, the different types of commodities available for investment, and the risks associated with commodity investing.

Benefits of Investing in Commodities

Diversification: One of the primary benefits of investing in commodities is diversification. Commodities have a low correlation with traditional asset classes like stocks and bonds, which means they tend to perform differently in different market conditions. This makes them a valuable addition to a portfolio as they can help reduce overall portfolio volatility and improve risk-adjusted returns.

Inflation Protection: Commodities are also a good hedge against inflation. Inflation erodes the purchasing power of currency over time, but the prices of commodities tend to rise with inflation. As a result, investing in commodities can help protect against the loss of value that occurs with inflation.

Supply and Demand Dynamics: Commodities are driven by supply and demand dynamics. When demand for a commodity increases, its price tends to rise, and when supply decreases, its price tends to rise. As a result, commodity prices can be highly responsive to changes in global economic conditions and geopolitical events.

Types of Commodities Available for Investment

There are several different types of commodities available for investment, including:

1. Precious Metals: Precious metals like gold and silver are highly valued for their rarity, durability, and use in jewelry, coins, and industrial applications. These metals are often viewed as safe-haven assets during times of economic uncertainty and are popular among investors looking to hedge against inflation and diversify their portfolios.

2. Energy: Energy commodities like oil and natural gas are essential to modern economies and are used to fuel transportation, manufacturing, and electricity generation. These commodities are highly responsive to changes in global economic conditions and geopolitical events, which can lead to significant price volatility.

3. Agriculture: Agricultural commodities like corn, wheat, and soybeans are used as food and feed for livestock. These commodities are highly responsive to weather conditions, global supply and demand, and government policies.

4. Industrial Metals: Industrial metals like copper, aluminum, and zinc are used in manufacturing and construction. These commodities are highly responsive to

changes in global economic conditions and are often viewed as leading indicators of economic activity.

Risks Associated with Commodity Investing

Like any investment, commodity investing comes with its own set of risks. Some of the risks associated with commodity investing include:

1. Volatility: Commodities are known for their high levels of price volatility, which can be challenging for investors to manage. Prices can be impacted by a wide range of factors, including changes in supply and demand, geopolitical events, and weather patterns.

2. Storage and Transportation Costs: Unlike stocks and bonds, commodities require physical storage and transportation, which can add to the cost of investing in these assets. Additionally, storage costs can vary depending on the commodity and the location, making it difficult to accurately estimate the total cost of investment.

3. Counterparty Risk: Commodities are often traded through futures contracts, which come with counterparty risk. This risk arises when one party to the contract defaults on their obligations, which can result in losses for the other party.

4. Political Risk: Commodities can be highly sensitive to changes in government policies and regulations, particularly in developing countries. Political instability can lead to disruptions in supply and demand, which can impact commodity prices.

Conclusion

Investing in physical commodities can be a valuable addition to a well-diversified investment portfolio. Commodities provide a hedge against inflation and can offer diversification benefits due to their low correlation with traditional asset classes like stocks and bonds. Additionally, the supply and demand dynamics of commodities can provide opportunities for attractive returns for investors.

When investing in commodities, it is essential to consider the risks associated with these assets. Price volatility, storage and transportation costs, counterparty risk, and political risk are all factors that investors must be aware of when considering a commodity investment.

One way to invest in commodities is through exchange-traded funds (ETFs), which provide exposure to a broad range of commodities and can offer investors a more cost-effective and diversified approach to commodity investing. Another option is to invest directly in physical commodities, such as gold bullion or agricultural products, which can be purchased through specialized dealers.

It is important for investors to do their due diligence when considering a commodity investment and to have a clear understanding of the risks and potential rewards associated with these assets. Working with a financial advisor or investment professional can help investors navigate the complex world of commodity investing and build a diversified investment portfolio that meets their unique needs and objectives.

In summary, investing in physical commodities can be a valuable strategy for diversifying investment portfolios and protecting against inflation. Precious metals, energy, agriculture, and industrial metals are all types of commodities available for investment, each with its own set of unique risks and potential rewards. While commodity investing can be challenging, it can also offer attractive returns for investors willing to do their homework and manage the risks associated with these assets.

Chapter 12. Gold
A Safe Haven Investment in Times of Economic Uncertainty

Introduction

Gold has long been considered a safe haven investment in times of economic uncertainty. It is a tangible asset that has stood the test of time and has been valued by people for centuries. While the price of gold may fluctuate, it has consistently proven to hold its value over the long term. In this article, we will explore why gold is considered a safe haven investment, the historical performance of gold during times of economic uncertainty, and how to invest in gold.

Why is Gold Considered a Safe Haven Investment?

Gold is considered a safe haven investment for several reasons. Firstly, it is a tangible asset that can be held and stored physically. This means that it is not dependent on any other party, such as a bank or government, for its value. It is also not subject to the same risks as other financial assets such as stocks and bonds, which can be affected by market fluctuations and changes in interest rates.

Secondly, gold has a limited supply. Unlike paper currency, which can be printed at any time, gold is a finite resource. The amount of gold in the world is limited, which means that its value is less susceptible to inflation than paper currency.

Thirdly, gold is seen as a form of currency that is universally accepted. It is traded around the world and is not tied to any particular country or currency. This makes it a valuable asset to hold in times of political and economic instability.

Historical Performance of Gold During Times of Economic Uncertainty

Gold has a long history of performing well during times of economic uncertainty. For example, during the 2008 financial crisis, when stock markets around the world were crashing, the price of gold rose sharply. Between 2007 and 2011, the price of gold increased by over 250%. This was because investors were looking for a safe haven to store their wealth, and gold was seen as a reliable option.

Similarly, during the COVID-19 pandemic, the price of gold rose to a seven-year high. This was because investors were once again seeking a safe haven to store their wealth as the global economy struggled to cope with the pandemic.

Gold has also performed well during times of high inflation. In the 1970s, when inflation in the United States was soaring, the price of gold rose from around $35 per ounce to over $800 per ounce in just a few years. This was because investors were seeking a store of value that would hold its worth as the value of paper currency declined.

How to Invest in Gold

There are several ways to invest in gold, each with its own advantages and disadvantages.

Physical Gold

One way to invest in gold is to purchase physical gold, such as gold bars or coins. This has the advantage of providing tangible ownership of the asset, which can be reassuring for some investors. However, there are also several disadvantages to investing in physical gold. Firstly, storing physical gold can be expensive and risky. Investors need to take precautions to ensure that their gold is stored securely, which can be costly. Secondly, buying and selling physical gold can be more difficult than other forms of investment. Investors may need to pay a premium to purchase gold and may receive less than market value when they sell it.

Gold ETFs

Another way to invest in gold is through exchange-traded funds (ETFs) that track the price of gold. Gold ETFs offer investors exposure to the price of gold without having to physically own the asset. This has several advantages, such as lower transaction costs and greater liquidity. However, ETFs are still subject to market fluctuations and may not provide the same level of security as physical gold.

Gold Mining Stocks

Investors can also invest in gold mining stocks. These are shares in companies that mine gold. The advantage of investing in gold mining stocks is that they offer exposure to the price of gold, while also providing the potential for growth through the company's operations. However, gold mining stocks can be more volatile than physical gold or gold ETFs, as they are subject to additional risks such as operational and geopolitical risks.

Gold Futures and Options

Investors can also invest in gold futures and options, which are contracts that allow them to buy or sell gold at a specific price at a future date. Futures and options trading can provide opportunities for high returns, but it is also considered a more advanced form of investing. It requires a deep understanding of the markets and the ability to manage risk effectively.

Conclusion

In times of economic uncertainty, gold has consistently proven to be a safe haven investment. Its tangible nature, limited supply, and universal acceptance have made it a valuable asset for investors looking to store their wealth securely. While the price of gold may fluctuate in the short term, its historical performance during times of economic turmoil and inflation make it a compelling option for long-term investors. When considering investing in gold, it is important to understand the different investment options available and to choose the one that best suits your investment goals and risk tolerance.

Chapter 13. Forex Trading
Investing in Foreign Currencies

Introduction

The foreign exchange market, commonly known as forex or FX, is the largest and most liquid financial market in the world. With an average daily turnover of over $6.6 trillion, it is a popular investment option for traders and investors looking to profit from fluctuations in the value of different currencies.

Forex trading involves buying and selling currencies in pairs, with the aim of profiting from changes in their exchange rates. This article will provide an overview of forex trading, its benefits and risks, and some tips for beginners looking to get started.

What is Forex Trading?

Forex trading involves buying and selling currencies in pairs, with the aim of profiting from changes in their exchange rates. For example, if you believe that the Euro will appreciate against the US dollar, you would buy the EUR/USD currency pair. If your prediction is correct and the Euro does indeed appreciate, you can sell the Euro back for a profit.

Forex trading is conducted over-the-counter (OTC) through a network of banks, financial institutions, and individual traders. There is no central exchange, and trading takes place 24 hours a day, five days a week. This means that traders can participate in the market from anywhere in the world, at any time.

Benefits of Forex Trading

1. High liquidity: Forex is the most liquid financial market in the world, with a high volume of transactions occurring on a daily basis. This means that traders can easily enter and exit trades, without worrying about liquidity issues.

2. Low barriers to entry: Unlike other financial markets, such as stocks or commodities, forex trading requires relatively little capital to get started. Most brokers allow traders to open accounts with as little as $100.

3. 24-hour trading: The forex market is open 24 hours a day, five days a week, allowing traders to participate in the market at any time.

4. Diversification: Forex trading allows investors to diversify their portfolios, by adding exposure to different currencies and markets.

5. Leverage: Forex brokers offer traders the ability to trade on margin, which means that they can control larger positions with smaller amounts of capital. This can magnify profits, but also increases the risk of losses.

Risks of Forex Trading

1. High volatility: Forex prices can be highly volatile, and can change rapidly in response to economic and political events. This can result in large gains or losses, depending on the direction of the price movement.

2. Leverage: While leverage can magnify profits, it also increases the risk of losses. Traders can quickly lose their entire investment if the market moves against them.

3. Counterparty risk: Forex trading is conducted over-the-counter, which means that there is a risk that the counterparty to a trade may default on their obligations.

4. Regulatory risk: Forex trading is not regulated in all countries, which can increase the risk of fraud and malpractice.

5. Complexity: Forex trading can be complex, and requires a good understanding of economic and geopolitical factors that can affect currency prices.

Tips for Beginners

1. Learn the basics: Before getting started with forex trading, it is important to learn the basics of the market, including how it works, the different types of currency pairs, and the factors that can affect currency prices.

2. Choose a reliable broker: When choosing a forex broker, it is important to choose a reputable and reliable broker, with a good track record and a strong regulatory framework.

3. Develop a trading plan: Before placing any trades, it is important to develop a trading plan, which includes your goals, risk tolerance, and trading strategy.

4. Start small: When getting started with forex trading, it is important to start with a small amount of capital, and to gradually increase your investment as you gain experience and confidence in your trading abilities.

5. Manage your risks: It is important to manage your risks when trading forex, by using stop-loss orders, limiting your leverage, and diversifying your portfolio.

6. Keep up-to-date with market news: Economic and geopolitical events can have a significant impact on currency prices. It is important to stay up-to-date with market news and events, and to adjust your trading strategy accordingly.

7. Practice with a demo account: Most forex brokers offer demo accounts, which allow traders to practice trading in a simulated environment, without risking real money. This is a great way to gain experience and test out different trading strategies, without incurring any financial risk.

Conclusion

Forex trading can be a lucrative investment option, for those with a good understanding of the market and the risks involved. However, it is important to approach forex trading with caution, and to manage your risks carefully. By choosing a reliable broker, developing a trading plan, and staying up-to-date with market news, you can increase your chances of success in the forex market.

Chapter 14. Cryptocurrency

An Overview of Investing in Digital Assets

Introduction

Cryptocurrency, also known as digital assets, has become increasingly popular over the past decade. Bitcoin, the first cryptocurrency, was created in 2009, and since then, many other digital currencies have been introduced. The market capitalization of all cryptocurrencies is now in the trillions of dollars, making them a legitimate asset class. This article will provide an overview of investing in digital assets, including the advantages and disadvantages of investing in cryptocurrency, how to invest in cryptocurrency, and some of the risks involved.

Advantages of Investing in Cryptocurrency

One of the primary advantages of investing in cryptocurrency is its decentralization. Cryptocurrencies are not controlled by any government or financial institution, which means that they are not subject to the same regulations as traditional investments. This can be a significant advantage for investors who want to avoid government interference and want to invest in a truly global market.

Another advantage of investing in cryptocurrency is its transparency. All transactions on a blockchain are public, which means that investors can see exactly where their money is going. This transparency can help to prevent fraud and increase trust in the market.

Cryptocurrencies are also highly liquid, which means that they can be bought and sold quickly and easily. This makes them an attractive investment for traders who want to take advantage of short-term price movements.

Finally, cryptocurrencies are highly secure. Transactions on a blockchain are protected by complex algorithms that are virtually impossible to hack. This means that investors can have confidence in the security of their investment.

Disadvantages of Investing in Cryptocurrency

While there are many advantages to investing in cryptocurrency, there are also several disadvantages. One of the primary disadvantages is volatility. Cryptocurrencies are highly volatile and can experience significant price swings in a short period of time. This can make them a risky investment, especially for those who are not willing to tolerate the risk.

Another disadvantage of investing in cryptocurrency is its lack of regulation. While the lack of regulation can be an advantage, it can also be a disadvantage. Without regulation, there is a higher risk of fraud and scams, which can lead to significant losses for investors.

Finally, cryptocurrency is still a relatively new investment, and there is a significant amount of uncertainty around its future. While many investors believe that cryptocurrency has significant potential, there is still a lot of uncertainty around how the market will develop over the long term.

How to Invest in Cryptocurrency

Investing in cryptocurrency can be a complex process, but there are several steps that investors can take to get started. The first step is to choose a cryptocurrency exchange. There are many exchanges available, each with its own advantages and disadvantages. Investors should research each exchange carefully before choosing one.

Once an exchange has been chosen, investors will need to set up an account and deposit funds. Most exchanges accept deposits in fiat currency, such as US dollars or Euros. Once the funds have been deposited, investors can then buy and sell cryptocurrencies on the exchange.

It is important to note that cryptocurrency exchanges are not regulated in the same way as traditional financial institutions. This means that investors should be careful when choosing an exchange and should take steps to protect their investment.

Risks of Investing in Cryptocurrency

There are several risks involved in investing in cryptocurrency. One of the primary risks is volatility. Cryptocurrencies are highly volatile and can experience significant price swings in a short period of time. This can make them a risky investment, especially for those who are not willing to tolerate the risk.

Another risk of investing in cryptocurrency is the lack of regulation. Without regulation, there is a higher risk of fraud and scams, which can lead to significant losses for investors.

Finally, cryptocurrency is still a relatively new investment, and there is a significant amount of uncertainty around its future. While many investors believe that cryptocurrency has significant potential, there is still a lot of uncertainty around how the market will develop over the long term. This uncertainty can make it difficult for investors to make informed investment decisions.

In addition to these risks, there are also several technical risks associated with investing in cryptocurrency. One of the primary technical risks is the risk of a blockchain attack. A blockchain attack occurs when a hacker gains control of a significant portion of a cryptocurrency network, which can result in the theft of large amounts of cryptocurrency.

Another technical risk is the risk of a coding error in the cryptocurrency's protocol. If a coding error is discovered, it can result in a significant loss of value for the cryptocurrency.

Finally, there is the risk of losing access to cryptocurrency due to a lost password or key. Unlike traditional investments, cryptocurrency is stored in digital wallets that require a password or key to access. If an investor loses their password or key, they can lose access to their cryptocurrency, which can result in significant losses.

Tips for Investing in Cryptocurrency

Despite the risks associated with investing in cryptocurrency, there are several tips that investors can follow to minimize their risk. The first tip is to do thorough research before investing. Investors should research the cryptocurrency they are interested in, the exchange they plan to use, and the potential risks involved.

Another tip is to invest only what you can afford to lose. Cryptocurrency is a highly volatile investment, and investors should be prepared for the possibility of losing their investment.

Investors should also be careful when choosing an exchange. They should choose an exchange that is reputable, secure, and has a good track record.

Finally, investors should consider diversifying their cryptocurrency portfolio. Investing in multiple cryptocurrencies can help to minimize risk and increase the potential for returns.

Conclusion

Cryptocurrency is a relatively new investment that has become increasingly popular over the past decade. While there are many advantages to investing in cryptocurrency, there are also several risks involved. Investors should carefully consider the potential risks and rewards before investing in cryptocurrency.

Investing in cryptocurrency can be a complex process, but by following a few simple tips, investors can minimize their risk and increase their potential for returns. As the cryptocurrency market continues to grow and evolve, it is likely that more investors will begin to see the potential benefits of investing in digital assets.

Chapter 15. Invoice Discounting

A Smart Way to Invest in Small Business Financing

Introduction

Invoice discounting is a smart way for small businesses to access financing. It involves selling invoices to a third-party financier in exchange for immediate cash. The financier pays a percentage of the invoice value upfront and collects the full amount from the customer later. This allows small businesses to receive funds quickly, improving their cash flow and enabling them to invest in growth opportunities.

In this article, we will explore the concept of invoice discounting, its benefits for small businesses, and how it works in practice. We will also discuss some of the potential risks and considerations that businesses should be aware of before using this financing option.

What is Invoice Discounting?

Invoice discounting is a type of financing where a third-party financier purchases outstanding invoices from a business at a discount. The financier pays a percentage of the invoice value upfront, typically between 70% to 90%, and collects the full amount from the customer when the invoice is due.

This financing option is particularly useful for small businesses that have outstanding invoices with long payment terms. Waiting for payment can create cash flow problems, limiting a business's ability to invest in growth opportunities or pay suppliers and employees on time. Invoice discounting solves this problem by providing immediate cash, enabling businesses to access funds without waiting for customers to pay.

Benefits of Invoice Discounting for Small Businesses

1. Improved Cash Flow

Invoice discounting enables small businesses to access funds quickly, improving their cash flow. This allows businesses to pay suppliers and employees on time, invest in growth opportunities, and avoid cash flow problems that can limit their ability to operate effectively.

2. Flexible Financing

Unlike traditional bank loans, invoice discounting is a flexible financing option that can be used as and when needed. Businesses can choose which invoices to sell and when to sell them, giving them greater control over their finances.

3. Lower Risk

Invoice discounting is a lower-risk financing option compared to other forms of financing, such as loans. The financing is secured against the value of outstanding invoices, reducing the risk for the financier. This can also result in lower interest rates for the business.

4. Increased Working Capital

By providing immediate cash, invoice discounting can increase a business's working capital. This can be used to invest in growth opportunities, pay suppliers and employees on time, and improve the overall financial health of the business.

How Does Invoice Discounting Work?

Invoice discounting works by following these basic steps:

1. A business raises an invoice and sends it to their customer.

2. The business sells the invoice to a third-party financier at a discount.

3. The financier pays the business a percentage of the invoice value upfront, typically between 70% to 90%.

4. The financier collects the full amount from the customer when the invoice is due.

5. The financier pays the remaining percentage of the invoice value to the business, minus their fee.

In practice, the process of invoice discounting can vary depending on the specific terms of the agreement between the business and the financier. Some financiers may require businesses to meet certain criteria, such as a minimum invoice value or a certain level of creditworthiness.

Risks and Considerations

While invoice discounting can be a useful financing option for small businesses, it is important to be aware of the potential risks and considerations. These include:

1. Cost

Invoice discounting can be more expensive than traditional bank loans, with fees ranging from 0.5% to 5% of the invoice value. It is important to carefully consider the costs involved before deciding to use this financing option.

2. Customer Relationships

Selling invoices to a third-party financier can potentially damage customer relationships. It is important to communicate clearly with customers and ensure that they are aware of the financing arrangement.

3. Credit Risk

Invoice discounting is secured against outstanding invoices, which means that if customers do not pay on time or become insolvent, the financier may not be able to collect the full amount owed. This can result in the business being liable for the outstanding amount, which can be detrimental to their financial health.

4. Legal Considerations

It is important to ensure that the invoice discounting agreement is legally binding and that both parties understand their obligations and rights under the agreement. Businesses should also be aware of any potential tax implications associated with invoice discounting.

5. Fraud

Invoice discounting can be susceptible to fraud, particularly if the business or customer is not reputable. It is important to carry out due diligence and work with reputable financiers to minimize the risk of fraud.

Conclusion

Invoice discounting can be a smart way for small businesses to access financing and improve their cash flow. By selling outstanding invoices to a third-party financier, businesses can receive immediate cash, enabling them to invest in growth opportunities and pay suppliers and employees on time. However, it is important to be aware of the potential risks and considerations associated with invoice discounting and to carefully consider the costs involved before deciding to use this financing option.

Overall, invoice discounting can be a valuable financing option for small businesses looking to improve their cash flow and access flexible financing. By working with reputable financiers and carefully managing customer relationships, businesses can mitigate the risks and maximize the benefits of this financing option.

Chapter 16. Peer-to-Peer (P2P) Lending

A New Way to Invest Your Money

Introduction

Peer-to-Peer (P2P) lending is a relatively new way to invest money that has gained significant traction in recent years. The concept is simple: individuals lend money to other individuals or businesses through online platforms. P2P lending platforms connect borrowers directly with investors, allowing them to bypass traditional financial institutions such as banks. This article will explore the advantages and disadvantages of P2P lending as well as provide some tips on how to invest in this innovative approach to investing.

What is Peer-to-Peer Lending?

Peer-to-Peer lending is a way for people to lend money to other people or businesses without the need for a traditional financial intermediary, such as a bank or credit union. Instead, investors lend money through online platforms that match borrowers with lenders. P2P lending platforms provide a marketplace where investors can lend money to borrowers, and the platform takes a small fee for facilitating the transaction.

Advantages of P2P Lending

One of the main advantages of P2P lending is the potential for higher returns compared to traditional investments such as stocks, bonds, and mutual funds. P2P lending investors can earn interest rates ranging from 5% to 15% or more, depending on the risk level of the borrower and the platform. This is significantly higher than the average returns on savings accounts or CDs, which typically offer less than 1% interest.

Another advantage of P2P lending is the ability to diversify your portfolio. Investors can choose to invest in a variety of loans with different risk levels, allowing them to spread their risk across multiple borrowers. This reduces the impact of any one borrower defaulting on their loan, as the investor's overall portfolio is not concentrated in one loan.

P2P lending also offers investors the opportunity to support individuals and small businesses that may not have access to traditional bank loans. This can be particularly appealing to investors who want to support their local community or invest in socially responsible projects.

Disadvantages of P2P Lending

While there are many advantages to P2P lending, there are also some risks and disadvantages to consider. One of the biggest risks is the potential for borrower default. While P2P lending platforms typically have strict underwriting standards to minimize the risk of default, there is still a chance that borrowers may default on their loans. In such a case, the investor may lose some or all of their investment.

Another potential disadvantage of P2P lending is the lack of liquidity. Unlike stocks or mutual funds, P2P loans are not traded on a public market, and there is no guarantee that the investor will be able to sell their investment if they need to liquidate their assets. This means that P2P lending should be considered a long-term investment, and investors should not invest money that they may need in the short term.

Finally, P2P lending platforms are not currently regulated by the Securities and Exchange Commission (SEC), which means that investors may not have the same protections as they would with a traditional investment. This lack of regulation can make P2P lending riskier than other investments.

Tips for Investing in P2P Lending

If you are interested in investing in P2P lending, there are several tips to keep in mind to help you make the most of your investment:

1. Do your research: Before investing in any P2P lending platform, it is important to research the platform's history, track record, and underwriting standards. Look for reviews from other investors and check the platform's Better Business Bureau rating.

2. Diversify your portfolio: As with any investment, it is important to diversify your portfolio to minimize risk. Invest in a variety of loans with different risk levels to spread your risk across multiple borrowers.

3. Start small: It is always a good idea to start with a small investment and gradually increase your investment as you become more comfortable with the platform and the risks involved.

4. Monitor your investments: Keep a close eye on your investments and monitor them regularly. If you notice any issues or red flags, take action immediately.

5. Be aware of taxes: P2P lending income is generally taxable, so be sure to factor in taxes when considering your

returns. Consult with a tax professional for advice on how to minimize your tax liability.

6. Consider the fees: P2P lending platforms typically charge a fee for facilitating the transaction. Be sure to factor in these fees when calculating your potential returns.

7. Understand the risks: P2P lending is not a risk-free investment, and there is always a chance that borrowers may default on their loans. Make sure you understand the risks involved before investing.

Conclusion

Peer-to-Peer (P2P) lending offers investors a new way to invest their money, with the potential for higher returns compared to traditional investments. While there are risks involved, such as the potential for borrower default and lack of liquidity, P2P lending can be an attractive option for investors who are willing to take on some risk in exchange for potentially higher returns. If you are interested in investing in P2P lending, be sure to do your research, diversify your portfolio, monitor your investments, and understand the risks involved.

Chapter 17. Alternative investments

Hedge funds, private equity, and venture capital

Introduction

Alternative investments are a category of investments that lie outside the traditional realm of stocks, bonds, and cash. These assets can be classified as tangible or intangible and generally offer a range of investment opportunities that may not be available in traditional investments. Alternative investments have been gaining popularity over the past few decades, as investors seek to diversify their portfolios, increase returns, and manage risk.

Some of the most common alternative investments include hedge funds, private equity, and venture capital. These investment vehicles are often referred to as alternative asset classes, as they offer exposure to assets that are not readily accessible to individual investors or are difficult to trade in public markets.

In this article, we will delve into the world of alternative investments, focusing on hedge funds, private equity, and venture capital. We will explore what these investment vehicles are, how they work, and the risks and rewards associated with investing in them.

Hedge Funds

Hedge funds are a type of investment vehicle that pools money from high-net-worth individuals and institutional investors to invest in a wide range of assets, including stocks, bonds, derivatives, and commodities. Unlike traditional mutual funds, hedge funds are not subject to the same regulatory requirements, and as a result, they are able to pursue more aggressive investment strategies.

One of the defining features of hedge funds is their use of leverage. By borrowing money to invest in assets, hedge funds can amplify their returns. However, this also means that hedge funds can incur significant losses if their investments perform poorly. As a result, hedge funds tend to be riskier than traditional investments and are often only suitable for sophisticated investors who can tolerate higher levels of risk.

Hedge funds are also known for their use of alternative investment strategies, such as short selling, arbitrage, and hedging. These strategies enable hedge funds to generate returns in both up and down markets, and they are often used to generate absolute returns rather than benchmark-relative returns.

Private Equity

Private equity is a type of investment that involves investing in private companies or buying public companies and taking them private. Private equity firms raise funds from institutional investors, such as pension funds, endowments, and high-net-worth individuals, and use that money to invest in companies.

Private equity investments are typically made with a long-term horizon, often with the aim of improving the operations of the company and increasing its value over time. Private equity firms often take an active role in the management of the companies they invest in, working closely with management teams to implement operational improvements, streamline processes, and identify growth opportunities.

Private equity investments can offer significant returns, but they also carry significant risk. Private equity investments are illiquid, meaning that they cannot be easily bought or sold on public markets. This can make it difficult for investors to exit their investments if they need to access their capital. Additionally, private equity investments are often subject to high fees and expenses, which can eat into returns.

Venture Capital

Venture capital is a type of private equity investment that focuses on investing in early-stage companies with high growth potential. Venture capitalists typically invest in companies that are in their early stages of development, providing seed funding, Series A funding, and subsequent rounds of funding as the company grows.

Venture capital investments are generally high-risk, high-reward investments. Many early-stage companies fail, but those that succeed can offer significant returns to investors. Venture capitalists often take an active role in the management of the companies they invest in, providing advice, strategic guidance, and access to networks and resources.

Venture capital investments are often illiquid, and like private equity investments, they can be subject to high fees and expenses. However, they can also offer significant tax benefits to investors, as some countries offer tax breaks for investments in early-stage companies.

Risks and Rewards

While alternative investments such as hedge funds, private equity, and venture capital offer unique opportunities for investors, they also come with significant risks and rewards.

Rewards

The potential rewards of alternative investments can be significant. Hedge funds, private equity, and venture capital investments often offer higher returns than traditional investments, as they have the potential to generate alpha or excess returns above market benchmarks.

For example, hedge funds may employ sophisticated investment strategies to generate positive returns even in down markets. Private equity investments may offer significant upside potential if the company is successfully turned around or sold for a profit. Venture capital investments may provide access to high-growth companies in their early stages, offering the potential for significant returns as the company grows and matures.

In addition to potential higher returns, alternative investments may also offer diversification benefits. Because they are not correlated with traditional investments, alternative investments can help to reduce portfolio risk by spreading investments across multiple asset classes.

Risks

Alternative investments also come with significant risks. These investments are often illiquid, meaning that they cannot be easily bought or sold on public markets. This lack of liquidity can make it difficult for investors to exit their investments if they need to access their capital.

Additionally, alternative investments are often subject to high fees and expenses. Hedge funds, private equity, and venture capital funds typically charge management fees of 1-2% of assets under management and performance fees of 20% of profits, known as a "2 and 20" fee structure. These fees can eat into returns and reduce the overall profitability of the investment.

Alternative investments are also generally riskier than traditional investments. Hedge funds, for example, may use leverage to amplify returns, but this also increases the risk of significant losses. Private equity and venture capital investments are also subject to significant risk, as many early-stage companies fail and investments may be illiquid for years.

Due diligence is critical when considering an investment in alternative assets. Investors should carefully review the investment strategy, track record, and fee structure of any investment opportunity, and consult with a financial advisor to determine whether the investment is suitable for their portfolio and risk tolerance.

Conclusion

Alternative investments such as hedge funds, private equity, and venture capital offer unique opportunities for investors seeking to diversify their portfolios, increase returns, and manage risk. These investment vehicles are often only accessible to high-net-worth individuals and institutional investors and are subject to higher fees and risks than traditional investments.

While alternative investments can offer significant rewards, they also come with significant risks. Due diligence is critical when considering an investment in alternative assets, and investors should carefully review the investment strategy, track record, and fee structure of any investment opportunity.

Ultimately, alternative investments may be a suitable addition to a well-diversified portfolio, but investors should consult with a financial advisor to determine whether these investments are appropriate for their individual needs and risk tolerance.

Chapter 18. Online Trading
A Beginner's Guide to Trading in Stocks and Shares

Introduction

Online trading has become increasingly popular in recent years, with more and more people turning to the internet to buy and sell stocks and shares. It has become a convenient and accessible way for individuals to participate in the stock market and potentially earn profits. However, for those who are new to online trading, it can seem like a daunting task. In this beginner's guide, we will discuss the basics of online trading and provide some tips for getting started.

What is Online Trading?

Online trading, also known as electronic trading, is the buying and selling of financial securities such as stocks, bonds, options, and futures through an electronic trading platform. This platform allows investors to place orders, monitor their investments, and execute trades through a computer or mobile device. Online trading has become popular due to its convenience, low fees, and ease of use.

Types of Securities

The stock market is a vast marketplace where investors can buy and sell securities. The most common types of securities traded online are stocks and shares. Stocks represent ownership in a company, and shares represent a portion of that ownership. When you buy a stock, you become a shareholder and are entitled to a portion of the company's profits.

Other types of securities that can be traded online include:

Bonds: A bond is a debt security issued by a company or government. When you buy a bond, you are lending money to the issuer, and they pay you interest in return.

Options: An option is a contract that gives the holder the right to buy or sell an asset at a certain price on or before a specified date.

Futures: A futures contract is an agreement to buy or sell an asset at a set price at a future date.

Choosing a Broker

To begin trading online, you will need to open an account with an online broker. A broker is a firm that provides access to a trading platform, research, and other tools that allow investors to buy and sell securities.

There are several factors to consider when choosing an online broker, including:

1. Fees: The fees charged by the broker for buying and selling securities can vary significantly. Some brokers charge a flat fee per trade, while others charge a percentage of the trade value. Look for a broker with transparent pricing and low fees.

2. Trading platform: The trading platform is the software that allows you to buy and sell securities. Look for a platform that is easy to use and has a range of tools for analysis and research.

3. Customer service: Choose a broker with good customer service. Look for a broker that offers support through phone, email, or live chat.

4. Security: Ensure that the broker you choose has strong security measures in place to protect your personal and financial information.

5. Reputation: Check the reputation of the broker by reading online reviews and checking with regulatory authorities. Look for a broker with a good reputation for customer service and reliability.

Opening an Account

Once you have chosen a broker, you will need to open an account. This typically involves filling out an online application and providing some personal and financial information. You may also be required to provide proof of identity and address.

After your application is approved, you can fund your account and begin trading. Most brokers allow you to fund your account using a bank transfer, credit card, or debit card.

Placing a Trade

To place a trade, log in to your trading account and select the security you wish to trade. You will then need to enter the number of shares you wish to buy or sell and the price at which you want to trade.

There are two types of orders: market orders and limit orders. A market order is an order to buy or sell a security at the current market price. A limit order is an order to buy or sell a security at a specified price or better.

It is essential to understand the risks involved in online trading. The stock market can be volatile, and prices can fluctuate rapidly. It is crucial to do your research and make informed decisions when buying and selling securities.

Tips for Successful Online Trading

1. Do your research: Before buying a security, research the company and the industry in which it operates. Look for news and trends that could affect the company's stock price.

2. Diversify your portfolio: Diversification can help reduce the risk of losses. Invest in a mix of stocks, bonds, and other securities to spread your risk.

3. Set realistic goals: Set realistic goals for your investments, and avoid chasing hot stocks or trying to time the market.

4. Use stop loss orders: A stop-loss order is an order to sell a security if it reaches a certain price. It can help limit losses if the market moves against you.

5. Keep an eye on fees: Fees can eat into your returns, so look for a broker with low fees and avoid frequent trading.

6. Stay disciplined: Stick to your investment plan and avoid making emotional decisions based on short-term market fluctuations.

Conclusion

Online trading can be a convenient and accessible way to invest in the stock market. However, it is essential to choose the right broker, do your research, and understand the risks involved. By following these tips, you can become a successful online trader and potentially earn profits from your investments. Remember to stay disciplined, diversify your portfolio, and set realistic goals for your investments.

Chapter 19. Investing in Bank Deposits
Pros and Cons

Introduction

Investing is a crucial aspect of financial planning that enables individuals to build their wealth and secure their financial future. There are various investment options available in the market, including stocks, mutual funds, real estate, and bank deposits. Among these options, bank deposits are considered a safe and secure way of investing money. In this article, we will discuss the pros and cons of investing in bank deposits.

Pros of Investing in Bank Deposits

1. Guaranteed Returns: One of the primary benefits of investing in bank deposits is that they offer guaranteed returns. Banks typically provide a fixed rate of interest on deposits, which remains constant throughout the investment tenure. This means that investors can calculate their returns in advance and plan their finances accordingly.

2. Safety and Security: Bank deposits are considered a safe and secure investment option as they are backed by the government. In case of bank failure, depositors are insured up to a certain amount by the Federal Deposit Insurance Corporation (FDIC) or the National Credit Union Administration (NCUA). This insurance ensures that depositors do not lose their money even if the bank fails.

3. Liquidity: Bank deposits offer high liquidity, which means that investors can withdraw their money anytime they want. This feature makes bank deposits an attractive

option for short-term investors who need quick access to their funds.

4. Low Risk: Bank deposits are considered a low-risk investment option as they are not subject to market fluctuations like stocks or mutual funds. This makes them a safe option for investors who are risk-averse or looking for a stable investment option.

5. Ease of Investment: Investing in bank deposits is easy and hassle-free. Investors can open a deposit account online or visit a bank branch to open an account. They can also set up automatic deposits to make regular contributions to their account.

Cons of Investing in Bank Deposits

1. Low Returns: One of the major drawbacks of investing in bank deposits is that they offer low returns compared to other investment options like stocks or mutual funds. The fixed rate of interest offered by banks may not keep up with inflation, which means that the real returns may be lower than expected.

2. Limited Options: Bank deposits offer limited investment options compared to other investment options. Investors can choose between fixed deposits and savings accounts, which may not offer much flexibility in terms of investment strategies.

3. Penalty for Early Withdrawal: Banks may impose penalties for early withdrawal of deposits, which can reduce the returns on investment. These penalties may vary depending on the bank and the investment tenure.

4. Tax Implications: Interest earned on bank deposits is subject to tax, which can reduce the overall returns on investment. Investors need to factor in the tax implications while calculating the returns on their investment.

5. Inflation Risk: Bank deposits are not immune to inflation risk, which means that the real value of the investment may decrease over time. This risk is higher for long-term deposits as the returns may not keep up with inflation.

Conclusion

Investing in bank deposits offers several benefits, including guaranteed returns, safety, and security, high liquidity, low risk, and ease of investment. However, there are also some drawbacks, such as low returns, limited options, penalties for early withdrawal, tax implications, and inflation risk. Investors need to weigh the pros and cons of investing in bank deposits and consider their investment goals and risk appetite before making a decision. They can also explore other investment options like stocks, mutual funds, or real estate to diversify their portfolio and maximize their returns.

Chapter 20. Insurance Policies
An Alternative Investment Avenue

Introduction

Investment is a crucial aspect of financial planning that helps individuals to grow their wealth over time. Traditional investment options such as stocks, mutual funds, and bonds are commonly known and utilized by people. However, insurance policies can also be considered as an alternative investment avenue. Insurance policies are generally seen as a tool to provide financial security to individuals in the event of any unfortunate occurrence. However, insurance policies can also be utilized to generate wealth and provide an alternative investment avenue. In this article, we will explore the various insurance policies that can be utilized as an investment avenue.

Types of Insurance Policies as Investment Avenue

Endowment Policies

Endowment policies are a type of insurance policy that provides a guaranteed return on the investment after a specific period. These policies are a combination of insurance and investment, where a portion of the premium paid is utilized to provide life coverage, and the rest is invested to generate returns. Endowment policies have a lock-in period of 5-10 years, and the policyholder receives the maturity amount at the end of the term. The returns on endowment policies are generally lower than other investment avenues, but they provide a guaranteed return and tax benefits under section 80C of the Income Tax Act (India).

Unit Linked Insurance Plans (ULIPs)

ULIPs are a type of insurance policy that provides both life coverage and investment opportunities (India). A portion of the premium paid is utilized to provide life coverage, and the rest is invested in the stock market or debt instruments. ULIPs offer the flexibility to choose the investment option and switch between them according to market conditions. The returns on ULIPs are market-linked and depend on the performance of the investment portfolio. ULIPs have a lock-in period of 5 years and offer tax benefits under section 80C and 10(10D) of the Income Tax Act (India).

Money-Back Policies

Money-back policies are a type of insurance policy that provides periodic payouts during the term of the policy. These policies provide life coverage and investment opportunities, where a portion of the premium paid is utilized to provide life coverage, and the rest is invested to generate returns. Money-back policies have a lock-in period of 5-25 years and provide periodic payouts during the term of the policy. The returns on money-back policies are generally lower than other investment avenues, but they provide a regular income stream and tax benefits under section 80C of the Income Tax Act (India).

Pension Plans

Pension plans are a type of insurance policy that provides regular income after retirement. These policies are designed to provide financial security to individuals after retirement. A portion of the premium paid is invested to generate returns, and the rest is utilized to provide life coverage. Pension plans have a lock-in period of 5-10 years and provide regular income after retirement. The returns on pension plans are generally lower than other investment avenues, but they provide a regular income stream and tax benefits under section 80CCC and 10(10A) of the Income Tax Act (India).

Benefits of Insurance Policies as an Investment Avenue

Diversification

Insurance policies provide an alternative investment avenue and help individuals to diversify their investment portfolio. Diversification helps to spread the risk and reduce the impact of market fluctuations on the overall investment portfolio.

Guaranteed Returns

Endowment policies and money-back policies provide guaranteed returns on the investment, which makes them a safe investment option. These policies offer a fixed rate of return, which helps individuals to plan their finances better.

Tax Benefits

Insurance policies offer tax benefits under section 80C, 80CCC, 10(10D), and 10(10A) of the Income Tax Act (India). These tax benefits help individuals to save taxes and increase their savings.

Life Coverage

Insurance policies also provide life coverage, which ensures that the family of the policyholder is financially protected in the event of the policyholder's untimely demise. The life coverage provides a sense of security to the policyholder and their family.

Regular Income Stream

Money-back policies and pension plans provide a regular income stream, which helps individuals to meet their regular expenses. These policies provide a fixed or variable income, depending on the investment portfolio's performance, which helps individuals to plan their finances better.

Flexibility

ULIPs offer the flexibility to choose the investment option and switch between them according to market conditions. This flexibility helps individuals to optimize their returns and reduce the impact of market fluctuations on their investment portfolio.

Risks Associated with Insurance Policies as an Investment Avenue

Lower Returns

The returns on insurance policies are generally lower than other investment avenues such as stocks and mutual funds. The returns are guaranteed but are lower than the market-linked returns provided by other investment avenues.

Lock-in Period

Insurance policies have a lock-in period, which means that the policyholder cannot withdraw their investment before the end of the term. This restricts the liquidity of the investment, and the policyholder cannot utilize the funds in case of any emergency.

Charges

Insurance policies come with various charges such as premium allocation charges, fund management charges, and mortality charges. These charges reduce the overall returns of the investment and should be considered while investing in insurance policies.

Conclusion

Insurance policies can be considered as an alternative investment avenue, which provides a safe and secure investment option. Endowment policies, ULIPs, money-back policies, and pension plans offer different investment opportunities and cater to different investment needs. Insurance policies provide diversification, guaranteed returns, tax benefits, life coverage, regular income stream, and flexibility. However, insurance policies also come with risks such as lower returns, lock-in period, and charges. Individuals should consider their investment needs and financial goals before investing in insurance policies as an investment avenue. It is always advisable to consult a financial advisor before making any investment decision.

Chapter 21. Retirement Planning

Investing for Your Future

Introduction

Retirement is an essential part of life. After years of hard work, everyone deserves a comfortable and stress-free retirement. However, it's crucial to start planning for retirement early to ensure that you can enjoy your golden years to the fullest. Investing is an excellent way to ensure financial security in retirement. In this article, we'll discuss retirement planning and the benefits of investing in different financial instruments.

Why Retirement Planning is Important

Retirement planning is essential for several reasons. First, life expectancy has increased over the years, and people are living longer than ever before. This means that you may need more money to support yourself during retirement. Additionally, the cost of living is increasing, and healthcare expenses are rising, making it even more crucial to have a solid retirement plan.

Secondly, relying solely on government programs like Social Security is not enough. Social Security benefits are only intended to provide a basic income, and you may need additional income to maintain your desired standard of living. Private pension plans are becoming less common, making it even more critical to save and invest for retirement.

Finally, retirement planning gives you peace of mind. Knowing that you have enough savings and investments to support yourself during retirement reduces financial stress and allows you to enjoy your retirement years to the fullest.

Starting Retirement Planning Early

The earlier you start retirement planning, the better off you'll be in the long run. Time is an essential factor in investing, and the earlier you begin investing, the more time your money has to grow. Additionally, starting early allows you to take advantage of compound interest, which means your investments earn interest on top of the interest they've already earned.

For example, suppose you invest $10,000 in a retirement account that earns an average annual return of 8%. After 20 years, your investment would be worth over $46,000. However, if you wait ten years to start investing, your investment would be worth just over $21,000 after 10 years. Starting early allows your investments to grow and compound over time, giving you a more significant return on your investment.

Investing in Stocks

One way to invest for retirement is to buy stocks. Stocks represent ownership in a company, and when a company performs well, the value of the stock increases. Investing in stocks is an excellent way to earn a high return on your investment, but it comes with higher risks.

The stock market is volatile, and prices can fluctuate rapidly. During the 2008 financial crisis, the stock market lost over 50% of its value in just 17 months. While the market has since recovered, this example illustrates the risks associated with investing in stocks.

However, history has shown that the stock market is an excellent long-term investment. According to the S&P 500 index, which tracks the performance of 500 of the largest publicly traded companies in the U.S., the average annual return over the last 100 years has been around 10%. While there are no guarantees that past performance will continue, investing in stocks can provide significant returns over the long term.

Investing in Bonds

Another way to invest for retirement is to buy bonds. Bonds are debt securities issued by corporations and governments, and they pay interest to investors. Unlike stocks, bonds are generally considered a lower-risk investment because they provide a predictable income stream and are less volatile than stocks.

However, bonds typically offer lower returns than stocks. The average annual return for bonds over the last 100 years has been around 5%. Additionally, inflation can erode the value of your investment over time. If inflation is higher than the interest rate on your bond, you'll lose purchasing power over time.

Investing in Mutual Funds

Mutual funds are an excellent way to invest in a diversified portfolio of stocks and bonds without having to choose individual stocks or bonds yourself. Mutual funds pool money from multiple investors and invest in a variety of securities based on a particular investment objective or strategy.

Mutual funds can be a good option for retirement planning because they offer diversification, which can help reduce risk. By investing in multiple securities, you're spreading your risk across different companies and industries. Additionally, mutual funds are professionally managed, which can help take the guesswork out of investing for those who are not familiar with the stock market.

However, mutual funds come with fees and expenses, which can eat into your investment returns. Make sure to research and compare different mutual funds to find one with low fees and expenses.

Investing in Real Estate

Investing in real estate can also be a good option for retirement planning. Real estate can provide a steady stream of income through rental properties, and property values can appreciate over time. Real estate can also offer tax benefits, such as depreciation deductions and tax-free exchanges.

However, investing in real estate can also come with risks. Property values can decline, and rental income may not cover the expenses of owning a property. Additionally, owning and managing rental properties can be time-consuming and require significant upfront costs.

It's essential to research and understand the real estate market before investing in property. Consider working with a professional real estate agent or property management company to help make informed investment decisions.

Creating a Retirement Plan

When creating a retirement plan, consider your retirement goals, timeline, and risk tolerance. Your retirement plan should outline how much money you'll need during retirement and how you plan to save and invest for that goal.

Consider using a retirement calculator to estimate how much money you'll need during retirement. A retirement calculator takes into account your current age, retirement age, estimated living expenses, and other factors to estimate your retirement needs.

Once you have an idea of how much you'll need during retirement, create a savings plan to help you reach your goal. Consider setting up automatic contributions to a retirement account, such as a 401(k) or IRA (applicable to United States), to ensure consistent savings.

Make sure to diversify your investments by investing in a mix of stocks, bonds, and other securities. This can help reduce risk and provide a more stable return on your investment. Consider working with a financial advisor to help create a retirement plan that fits your unique needs and goals.

Conclusion

Retirement planning is crucial for a stress-free and comfortable retirement. Investing in different financial instruments, such as stocks, bonds, mutual funds, and real estate, can help ensure financial security during retirement. Start planning early and consider your retirement goals, timeline, and risk tolerance when creating a retirement plan. Diversify your investments and consider working with a financial advisor to help make informed investment decisions.

"A Comprehensive Guide to Investment Opportunities" is a must-read for anyone looking to enter the world of investing. This book covers all the essential topics, including understanding the basics of investing, risk management, tax planning, and building a diversified investment portfolio. Readers will gain an in-depth understanding of investment options such as shares, bonds, mutual funds, exchange-traded funds, real estate, commodities, gold, forex trading, cryptocurrency, invoice discounting, peer-to-peer lending, alternative investments, online trading, investing in bank deposits, insurance policies, and retirement planning. This book is designed to provide readers with the knowledge and tools necessary to make informed investment decisions and maximize their returns while minimizing their risks.

ABOUT THE AUTHOR

Mr. C. P. Kumar is a retired Scientist 'G' from National Institute of Hydrology, Roorkee, Uttarakhand, India. He is also a Reiki Healer and Chakra Balancing practitioner (with pendulum dowsing) and offers Emotional Freedom Technique (EFT) to help individuals with emotional issues. Mr. Kumar has authored many books on technical, spiritual, and social topics.

For further details, you may visit his webpage https://www.angelfire.com/nh/cpkumar/virgo.html

www.ingramcontent.com/pod-product-compliance
Lightning Source LLC
LaVergne TN
LVHW022116200926
848481LV00003B/1177